CFD Trading for
Start Your Journey ~~to Financial~~ Success

Table of Contents

Table of Contents 1
Disclaimer 3
Objectives 4
Introduction to Financial Markets 5
   Understanding the Financial Ecosystem 5
Market Participants 6
The Role of CFDs in Financial Markets 7
Background 8
Benefits 10
Margins, Liquidations & Leverage 12
Margin Calls 13
Financing 15
Corporate Actions 16
Profits and Losses 19
Market Phases 21
Psychology of Trading 23
   Dealing with Loss 23
   The Importance of Discipline 23
   Avoiding Common Psychological Traps 25
Regulatory Environment and Compliance in CFD Trading
.... 26
   Importance of Trading with Regulated Providers 26
Regulatory Bodies and Regulations Across Jurisdictions
.... 27
   Compliance and Legal Implications 27
Building a Trading Plan 29
   Risk Management Strategies 29

Criteria for Entering and Exiting Trades 29
Future Outlook...32
Authors Note..36

Disclaimer

This educational material does not constitute a recommendation or opinion that an investment in certain financial products is appropriate for you, nor does it take into account your investment objectives, financial situation nor particular needs.

Before investing in any financial products, you must consider your objectives, financial situation and needs. Before you make any decision about acquiring a financial product, you should obtain and consider the relevant product disclosure statement. It is always recommended to use an independent advisor.

Objectives

This book aims to introduce the new CFD trader to the essential elements needed to trade. There are many aspects of CFD trading that may not be immediately obvious.

This book seeks to cover these areas, allowing the CFD trader to avoid some of the pitfalls while providing a strong foundation for their CFD trading.

A the end of this book you will understand

- The basic differences between CFDs and shares
- The impact of financing
- How corporate actions effect your portfolio
- The risks and benefits of leverage
- The importance of price depth
- How to place a range of orders
- How to trade a Sector or Index CFD
- CFD trading Dos and Don'ts

Introduction to Financial Markets

Understanding the Financial Ecosystem

Financial markets are complex systems where various participants come together to buy, sell, and trade financial instruments. These instruments can range from stocks, bonds, and currencies to derivatives such as futures, options, and Contracts for Difference (CFDs). At their core, financial markets serve two primary functions: price discovery and liquidity provision.

Price Discovery involves the process through which the prices of financial instruments are determined. It is a dynamic process that reflects the balance between supply and demand for assets, influenced by various factors including economic indicators, corporate performance, and geopolitical events.

Liquidity refers to the ease with which assets can be bought or sold in the market without causing significant changes in their prices. High liquidity is crucial for efficient markets, as it ensures that transactions can be executed quickly and at predictable prices.

Market Participants

The financial markets are populated by a diverse array of participants, each playing specific roles:

- **Retail Investors:** Individuals who invest their own money in various financial instruments, seeking to achieve personal financial goals such as savings, retirement, or income generation.

- **Institutional Investors:** Entities such as pension funds, mutual funds, and insurance companies that invest large sums of money on behalf of others. They have significant influence on market prices due to the size of their trades.

- **Traders:** Individuals or entities that buy and sell financial instruments with the aim of making profits from short-term price fluctuations. Traders can be further categorised into day traders, swing traders, and position traders, based on their trading horizon.

- **Market Makers:** Firms or individuals that provide liquidity to the market by continuously buying and selling financial instruments at publicly quoted prices. They profit from the spread between the buy and sell prices.

- **Brokers:** Intermediaries that facilitate transactions between buyers and sellers for a fee or commission. Brokers provide access to the financial markets and may offer additional services such as research, investment advice, and portfolio management.

- **Regulators:** Government or independent bodies that oversee the functioning of financial markets to protect investors, maintain fair, orderly, and efficient markets, and facilitate capital formation. Examples include the Securities and Exchange Commission (SEC) in the United States and the Financial Conduct Authority (FCA) in the United Kingdom.

The Role of CFDs in Financial Markets

Contracts for Difference (CFDs) are a type of derivative that allows traders to speculate on the price movements of financial instruments without owning the underlying assets. CFDs offer several advantages that make them a popular choice among traders:

- **Leverage:** CFD trading involves the use of leverage, allowing traders to open large positions with a relatively small amount of capital. This can amplify profits but also increases the risk of losses.

- **Market Access:** CFDs provide traders with easy access to a wide range of markets, including stocks, commodities, currencies, and indices, often through a single trading platform.

- **Going Short:** CFDs allow traders to take short positions, enabling them to profit from falling market prices as well as rising ones.

- **Cost Efficiency:** Trading CFDs often involves lower costs compared to buying the underlying asset directly. There are no stamp duties, and commissions are typically lower.

The use of leverage in CFD trading can also lead to significant losses, especially if the market moves against the trader's position. It is essential for traders to understand the risks involved and employ prudent risk management strategies.

Background

The use of Share CFDs date back to the 1980's when they were used by institutions to cost efficiently hedge their equity exposures. It wasn't until the late 1990's that they became available to private clients.

Nowadays, a growing number of retail investors use CFDs both as part of their trading portfolio and as an alternative to physical share trading. This group includes both short term frequent traders as well as long term investors looking for a flexible alternative to margin lending.

What are Share, Sector and Index CFDs

Contracts for Difference (CFDs) allow you to receive most of the benefits of owning a security without having to actually own the security. In other words you do not take delivery of the security so any difference in the price between when you buy the CFD and when you sell it is settled in cash. The difference is either profit or loss.

CFDs are also available on indices and baskets of securities. CFDs in relation to baskets of securities are known as Sector CFDs.

Buying and selling the performance of a security or index using a CFD is similar to buying the actual underlying instrument using a loan.

You could borrow $10,000 from a bank to buy shares. You would receive the returns from the shares, but would pay interest on the loan to the bank. CFDs combine this process in a single transaction.

For example, if you want to buy $10,000 worth of Australian shares you will have to deposit with your CFD provider as Initial Margin of

$1,000. You will then be allowed to purchase $10,000 worth of Share CFDs (based on a 10% initial margin percentage, though this percentage does vary).

The full $10,000 value of the Share CFDs will be subject to the share price performance.

If you want to keep the Share CFDs overnight you must pay a financing charge on the total notional value of the position at the Financing Rate. If a Share CFD position is not carried overnight you will pay no financing charge.

As with the underlying securities, Share CFDs allow you to benefit from normal market movements. Your open positions are valued every night at the close of business prices.

Profits or losses are credited / debited to your Account each day. Adjustments relating to corporate actions, such as dividends, bonus issues and reconstructions in respect of the underlying security are also applied to your account should they occur.

Benefits

Trade on Margin

CFDs are typically traded on margin, from 3% for Shares and 1% for indices. This is a more efficient use of your capital because you only have to allocate a small proportion of the total value of your position to secure a trade, while maintaining full exposure to the market. This enables you to magnify the returns on your investment.

Benefit from rising and falling markets

To go short means to open a position by first selling a CFD with the aim of profiting from a fall in its price. It is just as easy to sell short a Share, Index or Sector CFD as it is to buy.

Establishing a short position using a CFD is far easier than using physical shares. This is largely due to the Exchange regulations present in the physical market which do not apply in the CFD market. These regulations restrict the ways in which a physical share transaction can be executed. In particular, the "down-tick" rule prohibits an investor from selling a physical share into a falling market. With a CFD provider you have the ability to execute a short trade on any published price.

Going short in the physical market may also require a higher margin on the value of the position. CFD providers do not usually distinguish between a long and a short position in this regard.

Therefore, on this basis alone, a CFD is a more effective means for a trader to profit from falling markets (and short term intraday movements) and can also be used more easily to hedge long positions in the physical market.

Here is a selection of the key benefits of trading CFDs.

- Commissions are lower than the physical share market with some providers charging as little as $10 minimum or 0.1% for parcels over $10,000.
- Sectors and Indices are available with zero commission and 100 times leverage.
- 24 hour dealing desk and help desk.
- Lowest margin requirements with the many large cap stocks being offered at 3% margin.
- Free software that includes indicators, live data and backtesting software.
- Trade on the internet or over the phone and pay the same low brokerage.
- Open an account for as little as $1,000 (conditions apply).
- Place your stop and limit orders 24 hours a day online or over the phone.
- Low financing rates for all long positions allowing you maximum use of your cash.

Margins, Liquidations & Leverage

Margin and leverage are terms that are sometimes used interchangeably, but it is important to distinguish between them.

Margin is the amount of deposit required to secure a position. It ranges between 1% for Index and Sector CFDs and typically from 5 – 10% for individual Share CFDs.

The Margin is calculated as a percentage of the notional value of the position and is charged to cover the traders' account in the event that the position moves against them. The margin amount is returned to the trader when the position is closed out.

The Share CFD Margin requirement set by a CFD provider is determined by a range of factors including the liquidity of the underlying security and its capitalisation.

Leverage, also known as gearing, is the ability to take a position with notional value greater than the cash outlay required. For instance traditional share trading has leverage of 1:1. That is, for every $1 of investment the trader is required to pay $1 in cash. A Share CFD position with a 5% Margin requirement has leverage of 20:1. That means for every $1 of cash invested the profit or loss will be multiplied by factor of 20.

Other CFD products such as Index and Sector CFDs have a 1% margin which means leverage of 1:100. Leverage means returns are magnified and this applies equally to gains and losses.

Margin Calls

If the market moves against you and your equity balance falls below your Initial Margin you have the option to:

- close one or more of your open position(s), in order to reduce your Initial Margin to the required level; and/or

- remit further funds to your Account as deposit in order to maintain the Initial Margin.

This is the first trigger level for margin, referred to as the 'Margin Call'.

Before your equity falls below your Initial Margin requirement, it is advisable that you place a Stop-loss order with your CFD provider to try to avoid a deficit balance on your account.

Stop-out level

A CFD provider may place a Stop-loss order for your open position or positions, at a level where the total equity balance falls below the minimum equity balance. These levels are referred to as the "stop-out level" which is the second trigger level for margin.

At or below this level your CFD provider may close out all of your open positions. They may also place a stop-loss order for your open position or positions, at a level where the total equity balance falls below the stop-out level.

Once the stop-out level has been triggered, you may be restricted from dealing on your Account until the equity balance is restored to the required margin level.

However, it is important not to rely on your provider to close your positions. Further, there are no guarantees that your open positions will be closed out at any particular level. Accordingly, your losses may exceed the balance of your account.

Financing

If you hold your long Share, Index or Sector CFD position overnight and do not close it before the Settlement Time, you may incur a financing charge at the CMC Financing Rate, which would reduce your profit or increase your loss.

If you hold your short Share, Index or Sector CFD position overnight and do not close it before the Settlement Time, you may be credited an amount at the CMC Financing Rate, which would increase your profit or reduce your loss.

Example - Finance charge on NAB Long Example

The finance calculation is based on the current overnight rate plus a premium and is based on the full notional value of the position. It is deducted from the account on a daily basis

Lets say the current Central Bank rate is 5.25%, add 2% = 7.25%
Interest on long NAB position is calculated as: 1,000 x 27.50 x (7.25% / 360) = $5.53 per day

Example - Finance paid on NAB Short Example

The finance calculation for a short position is based on the current overnight rate minus a discount and is based on the full value of the position. It is deposited in the client account on a daily basis

Current Central Bank rate is 5.25%, less 2% = 3.25%
1,000 x 27.50 x (3.25% / 360) = $2.48 per day

NOTE: The Central Bank Rate can change at any time and the above demonstration is for illustration purposes only.

Corporate Actions

Corporate actions include dividend payments, rights issues, stock splits or mergers and acquisitions. These events and their effect on the underlying security or basket are reflected in the CFD market.

A dividend is treated as a cash adjustment to the client account. Stock splits and rights are either reflected in a cash adjustment or an adjustment to the size of the CFD position. Since a corporate action has the potential to effect a trader's bottom line a corporate actions calendar should be consulted before taking a position in a Share CFD.

Adjustments for Dividends

Long Share CFD position

If you have a long Share CFD position your Account will be adjusted for any Cash Dividend that the holder of the underlying security would have received after any tax has been paid or withheld by the issuer of that security. The adjustment will result in your Account being credited with an amount equal to the net amount of the Cash Dividend after such taxes have been taken into account.

The reference to Cash Dividend is to the cash dividend or distribution declared.
Accordingly, your Account is not adjusted for any Franking Credits attached to a dividend or distribution.

Short Share CFD position

If you have a short Share CFD position your Account may be adjusted for the grossed Up Dividend, being the sum of the Cash Dividend plus any Franking Credits attached to the

Cash Dividend. The adjustment will result in your Account being debited with an amount equal to the Grossed-up Dividend.

Timing of adjustments

CFD providers specify the time at adjustments are made to client Accounts. Usual practice is to align the CFD market with the physical market so that the value of the CFD position fully reflect the value of the underlying security.

Example - Dividend adjustment for BHP

At the end of June BHP is trading at $12.50 when the Board announces BHP will pay a 15 cent Dividend on July 21 to all security holders as at July 10 (the ex-dividend date).
The day before the ex-dividend date - July 9, BHP Share CFD holders, both long and shorts, will be registered by the CFD provider's back office to have their account adjusted for the dividend. Long positions receive the benefit and short positions have the benefit deducted.

The closing price for BHP is $12.75.

On the open of Jul 10 the share price typically falls in value an equivalent amount to reflect the distribution, i.e. by 15 cents to $12.60.

A trader with the 1000 BHP long position receives $150 (1,000 x 15c) at the end of the trading session on July 10. At the same time BHP shares are down 15c, which is a loss of $150. The net cash movement on the account is zero.

A trader with a short 1000 BHP position has $150 (1,000 x 15c) deducted from their account, but makes $150 from the share price movement. The net cash movement on the account is zero.

Suspended Share CFDs

When a company's security is suspended from trade on an Exchange, CFD providers will typically also suspend the CFD.

However, some CFD providers are market-makers and if they are able to value the CFD and provide an orderly market they may continue to quote a price for the CFD.

Suspensions may result from any of the following;

- A request by the Board pending a significant announcement which is expected to effect the security's price;

- A regulatory action being taken against the Company by either the Exchange or the corporate regulator;

- The announcement of a significant merger or acquisition involving the company; or

- The announcement of any information which could reasonably be expected to have an impact on the value of the Company's securities.

In these circumstances where there is significant uncertainty about the value of a security the CFD provider may increase the Margin requirement. In some cases, they may require 100% of the notional value of the position. It is important therefore that CFD traders take care not to overextend themselves.

Profits and Losses

All profits and losses are credited or debited to your Account in the currency in which the relevant CFD is denominated.

Market Depth

Market depth is the single most important facet of the CFD market for the new trader.
The Bid is the price at which the market is willing to purchase a Share CFD, while the Ask (or Offer) price is the price at which the markets is willing to sell a Share CFD. The Bid/Offer spread is a product of the best bid and offer in the market.

Market depth is a visual representation of the intentions of all buyers and sellers.
Table

The table is split into two sections: Buyers on the left and Sellers on the right. The first line is the highest Bid and lowest Offer and the respective volume available at those prices. The Bids and Offers – best to worst – are then listed below.

The best Bid and Offer prices on market depth are known as the 'touch price'.

Market depth broadly reflects the liquidity of a market. Liquidity is determined by the "depth" and "breadth" of the market. Depth refers to the range of prices and breadth means the amount of volume available at each price level. Therefore a liquid market will have a range of incremental prices with a high level of volume available at each price.

Market Capitalisation & Liquidity

Market capitalisation refers to the dollar value of the share capital of the company. A company with a large amount of issued capital that trades at a high price has a high capitalisation and is referred to as a "Large Cap" Stock.

Large Cap stocks such as global resource companies or Australia's biggest four banks will generally have greater liquidity and this will be reflected in the market depth.
Conversely, Small Cap stocks lack market depth.

Market Phases

There are three main market phases that are relevant to CFD traders - the open, midsession, and the close. The first trade price after the opening of the session in the underlying market determines the opening price for a Share CFD. Picking an opening price is nothing more than guess-work. A limit order left over the open may be filled at a better price or may not be filled at all. Market open can be characterised by high volatility and wide ranges.

Many securities exhibit reduced turnover throughout the middle of the trading session.

During these times liquidity generally falls and for this reason can be susceptible to single transactions. Inexperienced traders are often tempted to trade during this period.
Institutional dealers often remove orders over the lunchtime period.

Reflecting the share market, the CFD market can exhibit increased turnover and volatility in the last minutes of a trading session and on the close. At these times large market participants, for example Fund Managers and Trading Desks, will trade significant amounts to either balance their positions or support a market.

This is because the closing price is the price at which all CFDs and securities will be valued for income and balance sheet purposes. In the underlying market, after the close, an auction takes place between exchange members.

Generally the purpose of this auction is to provide Institutional traders a further opportunity to square their books. The CFD market does not reflect these transactions.

How to deal in Share CFDs

A position is opened by buying or selling CFDs:

- BUYING a CFD - To make a profit, you want the price of the underlying security, index or asset to rise.
- SELLING a CFD - To make a profit, you want the price of the underlying security, index or asset to fall.

A position is closed by you entering into an equivalent and offsetting position in the relevant Share CFD. Closing your position may result in a profit or loss being realised on your account.

You may close part of an open position by executing an equivalent and offsetting position of a lesser amount than the open position.

Psychology of Trading

Trading in the financial markets is not just about having a good strategy and understanding the market trends; it's also about mastering your own emotions. The psychology of trading plays a crucial role in your success or failure. Here's a look at some of the key psychological aspects you'll need to navigate as a trader, especially when dealing with Contracts for Difference (CFDs), which can amplify both gains and losses due to their leveraged nature.

Dealing with Loss

One of the most challenging aspects of trading is learning how to deal with loss. Losses are inevitable, even for the most seasoned traders. The key is not to avoid them but to manage them effectively. Here's how:

- **Acceptance:** Recognize that losses are part of the trading process. Accepting this reality helps in developing a more balanced approach to trading.

- **Emotional Resilience:** Building emotional resilience is crucial. Don't let a loss affect your confidence or decision-making in future trades.

- **Risk Management:** Implementing strict risk management rules can help minimise losses. This includes setting stop-loss orders and only risking a small percentage of your capital on any single trade.

The Importance of Discipline

Discipline is what separates successful traders from unsuccessful ones. It's about sticking to your trading plan, even when emotions are pulling you in different directions. Here's why discipline matters:

- **Consistency:** Discipline ensures that you trade consistently, following your strategy and analysis rather than whims or impulses.
- **Emotion Control:** By sticking to a plan, you're less likely to make trades based on fear, greed, or other emotions that can lead to irrational decisions.

- **Long-term Success:** Trading discipline helps in achieving long-term success, as it encourages adherence to proven strategies and risk management practices.

Avoiding Common Psychological Traps

Several psychological traps can ensnare traders, especially those new to the markets. Being aware of these can help you avoid them:

- **Overconfidence:** After a few successful trades, it's easy to become overconfident and take unnecessary risks. Remember, past success does not guarantee future results.

- **Fear of Missing Out (FOMO):** Watching others make money from market movements can lead to a fear of missing out. This can result in jumping into trades without proper analysis or strategy.

- **Anchoring:** This occurs when traders fixate on specific price points, such as the price at which they bought an asset, which can hinder the ability to make objective decisions.

- **Confirmation Bias:** Seeking out information that confirms your existing beliefs while ignoring contradictory evidence can lead to poor trading decisions.

Understanding and managing your emotions is as important as any trading strategy. The psychological challenges of trading CFDs are significant due to the potential for rapid gains and losses. By acknowledging these emotional aspects and implementing strategies to mitigate their impact, traders can improve their decision-making process, leading to more consistent and successful trading outcomes. Remember, trading is not just a test of your knowledge and skills but also a test of your emotional intelligence and discipline.

Regulatory Environment and Compliance in CFD Trading

Contracts for Difference (CFDs) are popular financial instruments that offer traders and investors the opportunity to profit from price movements without owning the underlying assets. However, the trading of CFDs is subject to strict regulatory environments across different jurisdictions. Understanding these regulations and the importance of compliance is crucial for traders to ensure they are trading legally and with the protection of regulatory frameworks.

Importance of Trading with Regulated Providers

Regulated CFD providers are overseen by financial authorities that enforce rules to protect investors, maintain fair markets, and promote financial stability. Here's why trading with a regulated provider is essential:

- **Investor Protection:** Regulated providers must adhere to standards that ensure the safety of client funds, such as segregating client money from their own funds and participating in compensation schemes.

- **Market Integrity:** Regulations help in maintaining the integrity of the financial markets by preventing manipulation, fraud, and other unethical practices.

- **Transparency:** Regulated providers are required to offer transparency regarding pricing, costs, and the risks associated with CFD trading, helping traders make informed decisions.

Regulatory Bodies and Regulations Across Jurisdictions

The regulatory environment for CFD trading varies significantly across different regions. Some of the key regulatory bodies and their regions include:

- **United States:** The trading of CFDs is not allowed for residents under current regulations enforced by the Commodity Futures Trading Commission (CFTC) and the Securities and Exchange Commission (SEC).

- **European Union:** The European Securities and Markets Authority (ESMA) has implemented measures including leverage limits, margin close-out rules, and negative balance protection to safeguard retail investors.

- **United Kingdom:** The Financial Conduct Authority (FCA) regulates CFD providers, imposing rules similar to ESMA, including leverage caps and ensuring that investors cannot lose more money than they have deposited.

- **Australia:** The Australian Securities and Investments Commission (ASIC) has introduced measures to protect retail clients, including restrictions on leverage, margin requirements, and implementing negative balance protection.

- **Asia:** Regulatory environments in Asia vary by country, with some allowing CFD trading under specific regulations, while others have more restrictive policies.

Compliance and Legal Implications

For traders, understanding the regulatory environment and ensuring compliance when trading CFDs is critical. Here are some implications of non-compliance:

- **Legal Risks:** Trading with unregulated providers or in jurisdictions where CFD trading is restricted or banned can expose traders to legal risks and the possibility of fraud.

- **Financial Risks:** Trading with providers that are not regulated by a reputable authority can increase the risk of unfair pricing, poor execution, and loss of funds due to lack of investor protection measures.

- **Reputation Risks:** Engaging in non-compliant trading activities can also affect a trader's reputation, especially if legal actions are taken against them.

The regulatory environment for CFD trading is designed to protect investors and ensure fair and transparent markets. Traders should prioritise trading with regulated providers and familiarise themselves with the rules and regulations applicable in their jurisdiction.

Building a Trading Plan

A well-structured trading plan is essential for achieving consistent success in the financial markets, especially in CFD trading, where the potential for high returns comes with high risk. A comprehensive trading plan serves as a roadmap, guiding your decisions based on predefined criteria rather than emotions. Here's how to develop one:

Risk Management Strategies

Risk management is the cornerstone of any successful trading plan. It involves identifying, assessing, and prioritising risks to ensure they are understood, managed, or mitigated. Here are key components:

- **Determine Risk Tolerance:** Assess your financial situation and risk appetite. How much of your portfolio can you afford to risk on CFD trading without affecting your financial stability?

- **Use Stop-Loss Orders:** A stop-loss order automatically closes out a trade at a predetermined price level to limit potential losses. It's a crucial tool for managing risk.

- **Set Risk-Reward Ratios:** Before entering a trade, decide on a risk-reward ratio that makes sense for your trading strategy and goals, such as 1:3, where for every dollar risked, the potential return is three dollars.

- **Diversify:** Avoid concentrating all your capital in a single trade or market. Diversification can help spread risk across different assets.

Criteria for Entering and Exiting Trades

Having clear criteria for when to enter or exit a trade helps prevent impulsive decisions driven by emotions.

- **Entry Criteria:** Define what conditions must be met before you enter a trade. This could include technical indicators, price patterns, or economic announcements that align with your trading strategy.

- **Exit Criteria:** Similarly, establish when you'll take profits or cut losses. This could be a specific profit target, a stop-loss level, or a change in market conditions that invalidates your trading premise.

Developing a Trading Strategy

Your trading strategy is the approach you take to market analysis and execution. It might be based on technical analysis, fundamental analysis, or a combination of both. The strategy should match your trading goals, time commitment, and risk tolerance.

Keeping a Trading Journal

A trading journal is a record of all your trades, including the strategy used, entry and exit points, outcomes, and any observations or lessons learned. Reviewing your journal regularly can provide valuable insights into your trading performance and areas for improvement.

Regular Review and Adjustment

Markets evolve, and so should your trading plan. Regularly review your trading goals, performance, and the effectiveness of your strategies. Be prepared to make adjustments based on new information or changes in your financial situation.

Building a comprehensive trading plan requires careful thought and ongoing refinement. It's about more than just deciding when to buy and sell; it's a holistic approach to trading that encompasses goal setting, risk management, and continuous learning. By adhering to a well-constructed trading plan, you can navigate the complexities of CFD trading with greater confidence and discipline, leading to improved decision-making and better overall performance.

Future Outlook

As we look toward the future of Contracts for Difference (CFD) trading, it's clear that this form of investment will continue to evolve alongside technological advancements and changing market dynamics. Emerging trends, such as the integration of artificial intelligence for market analysis and the development of more sophisticated risk management tools, promise to enhance the trading experience and potentially improve outcomes for traders.

The Future of CFD Trading

The digital transformation of financial markets is set to continue, with platforms becoming more user-friendly and accessible to a global audience. Additionally, regulatory landscapes across the world are likely to keep evolving, aiming to strike a balance between market freedom and investor protection. As a trader, staying informed about these changes and adapting your strategies accordingly will be crucial for success.

Staying Informed and Adapting to Market Changes

To navigate the future of CFD trading effectively, traders must commit to lifelong learning. This includes staying up-to-date with financial news, understanding global economic indicators, and continuously refining trading skills and strategies. Participating in trading communities, attending webinars, and following respected market analysts are all ways to stay informed and adaptable.

The Dangers of Leverage

A critical aspect of CFD trading that warrants repeated emphasis is the use of leverage. While leverage can amplify gains, it also significantly increases the risk of losses, potentially exceeding your initial investment. It's a powerful tool that should be used judiciously and in alignment with a well-thought-out risk management strategy. Your leverage level should not be dictated by the maximum offered by your provider but by the risk you are prepared to accept on each trade, as outlined in your trading plan.

Risk Management: The Key to Longevity

Having a robust risk management system is non-negotiable in CFD trading. This system should include setting stop-loss orders, determining appropriate risk-reward ratios, and never investing money you cannot afford to lose. The stories of traders who have lost their entire accounts serve as stark reminders of leverage's potential dangers. Your trading plan should clearly define how much risk you are willing to take on each trade, ensuring that you are in control of your exposure at all times.

The Dos and Don'ts

A trader should always have the price depth window open for the Share CFD they are trading. When trading at market the trader will always receive either the touch price, or you be requoted for the size a size larger than the current bid or offer.

Depth of market will change during the day. It is just an order book and generally does not offer any predictive qualities. However, if scanned with a trained eye, market depth can offer some form of insight into the collective opinion of the market.

Do not attempt to take on the order book. Remember for every buyer there is someone selling. If a trader was to strip all the size from two or three levels of market depth then other orders can quickly come in to fill the gaps which can push the position into a loss.

Avoid large positions in thinly traded CFDs. If a trader accumulates a large position in a Share CFD that typically has low liquidity, they will eventually have to exit the position. If the trader then attempts to dump a large volume on the market the position can potentially move the market in the opposite direction of the trade.

Don't bet the farm on one piece of news. In the Share CFD market, there is always "some big event" that might take place for a company or the market. Buying or selling based on the possibility that this event may or may not occur is gambling not trading.

Big corporate actions or corporate finance events such as mergers or acquisitions can get delayed for months or called off altogether.

Markets are not logical. A market will generally have moved well before the average individual hears about the news or even the rumour of the news. As a result, you may see stocks trade down on positive news due to the fact that the news was already anticipated long in advance and largely priced into the stock prior to the release of the actual news.

Avoid 'all your eggs in one basket' trading. Do not place all your CFD trading capital in one position. This is the equivalent of overtrading. Diversify your trading efforts. Think about spreading the market risk in your portfolio.

A Marathon, Not a Sprint

Remember, achieving long-term success in CFD trading is akin to running a marathon, not a sprint. It requires patience, discipline, and a continuous effort to improve. The allure of quick profits should not divert you from the path of strategic, informed trading. By respecting the market's power, understanding the tools and instruments you are working with, and committing to a disciplined approach to trading, you can navigate the complexities of CFD trading with confidence.

The journey of a trader is filled with learning and adaptation. By acknowledging the risks, especially those associated with leverage, and by diligently following a risk management plan, you position yourself for sustainable success. Good luck on your trading journey—remember, the path to achievement is a marathon, filled with both challenges and opportunities for growth.

Authors Note

As we reach the conclusion of this journey into the world of Contracts for Difference (CFD) trading, I hope you've found the insights, strategies, and advice shared within these pages both enlightening and practical. My aim has been not only to introduce you to the complexities of CFD trading but also to equip you with the knowledge and tools needed for navigating this dynamic market.

Share Your Experience

If this book has helped you in any way, or if you have suggestions for how it could be improved for future readers, I warmly encourage you to leave a review on Amazon. Your feedback is not only invaluable to me as an author but also helps other potential readers make informed decisions. Sharing your experience, thoughts, and the impact this book has had on your trading journey can make a significant difference.

Continue Your Learning Journey

The world of trading is vast, with endless opportunities for growth, learning, and exploration. If you're keen to delve deeper into trading strategies, market analysis, or other financial instruments, I invite you to explore my other books. Each one is crafted to address different facets of the financial markets, offering insights and guidance to enhance your understanding and skills.

You can find my complete collection of works by visiting my Author profile on Amazon. [Link to the author's profile will be provided here]

Whether you're looking to refine your approach to CFD trading, explore new markets, or deepen your understanding of financial analysis, there's a resource for you. My books cover a range of topics designed to support traders and investors at every stage of their journey, from beginners to more experienced market participants.

Final Words

Remember, success in trading is a marathon, not a sprint. It requires patience, discipline, and a commitment to continuous learning and improvement. The financial markets are always evolving, and so should your knowledge and strategies. I wish you the best of luck on your trading journey and hope to accompany you through my writings as you navigate the path to success.

Thank you for choosing this book.

Printed in Great Britain
by Amazon